The 30 Most Powerful Words in the English Language

By Roger W. Davis

Copyright © 2021 Roger W. Davis
All Rights Reserved.

To Marian

Thank you to three incredible editors.
Thank you for your feedback, inspiration,
and encouragement. My baby is finally in the world.

Thank you to:

Dr. Katie L. Thomas
Leslie R. Thompson
Jennifer Shields

Table of Contents

INTRODUCTION	1
JOY	6
FUN	9
CREATIVITY	12
CELEBRATION	15
FLY	18
CHILDHOOD	21
SUFFICIENCY	24
FAITH	27
MIRACLE	30
GOD	34
HELP	38
FORGIVENESS	41
GIVING	44
COMMITMENT	47
WORK	50
POWER	53
SEVEN	56
RISK	59
SLAVERY	62
CHOICES	65
LET	68
TIME	71
GRACE	73
FREEDOM	82
COVENANT	85
CHANGE	88
LIFE	94

INTRODUCTION

In the beginning was the word is written in the first chapter of John.

His final words, before he took his last breath, were...

After I proposed, I waited until I heard the word yes.

The prayer was filled with words of thanksgiving.

Her speech made the audience give her a standing ovation.

The word he used to describe her husband started the fight in the supermarket.

The lyrics to that song changed my life.

The business proposal received over $2 million in initial funding.

The attorney's closing arguments made the jury change their mind and find her innocent.

Words have power.

Language is the most powerful component of our humanity. Our words are the primary tool by which, we as humans, exchange information to communicate feelings, emotions, instructions, influence, assessment, and entertainment. Our words create a lens by which we see our world – past, present, and future. Words have the ability to shape our reality, our perception, our behaviors, and our emotions. If we want to improve our state of life, examine the words we use. Perhaps, our life status comes from the use, abuse, and misuse of language

In Vishen Lakhiani's book, *The Code of the Extraordinary Mind*, he writes about the Himba tribe and words that don't exist in their culture. In their native language, they have a word to describe the color green, but no word in their language for the color blue. When asked to identify one blue square among green squares, most of the tribe members struggled, took longer than usual or simply couldn't accomplish the task. However, when asked to identify a slightly different shade of green, they did it with ease. Lakhiani indicates what is easy for them (identifying a shade of green) would be hard of us and what is hard for them (identifying blue) would be easy for us. His conclusion is that language shapes what we see. In turn, I believe language can also shape how we feel, what we do, how we perform, and what we receive.

There have been several experiments in schools where students use words to see the effect on plants. On a daily basis, students speak negative words to one plant and positive words to another plant over a number of weeks. After a few days, the plant receiving positive feedback grows and the other plant receiving negative feedback begins to wilt and die. Using words over and over again, in this experiment, yielded growth and death.

Words have power.

From childhood to adulthood, when we want to learn or memorize something, we use repetition. In theater, we use repetition to remember script lines. In sports, we practice so we can build our muscle memory. To break a bad habit, we replace it with a different behavior for approximately 10 weeks to create a new habit. So, to change our life, I propose that we need to use language repetitively. Surround, immerse, and bathe yourself in positive, affirming, uplifting words on a daily basis.

When we use powerful language, we have the ability to shape and mold our life in a meaningful, abundant, and impactful way. Some of the most powerful words we use are the words we can use to describe ourselves. The power that it yields can also shape our world. Even in our darkest times, language can bring light to our situation and move us to action. Using powerful language has the ability to reprogram our thinking, our mindset, our psyche and ultimately renew us to our best self.

My editor, Dr. Katie Thomas, after reading the first draft, indicated that this book has a voice of a poet, a preacher, and a professor. I laughed because I have a degree in English. I was raised in the church. And I teach at the college level. So, as you read this book, you will find among the 30 words some that are used to inspire, others to motivate and others for empowerment. This book highlights the words that have moved my life foreword. I hope that the 30 words described, expounded upon, and dissected will speak to your creative, spiritual and academic mind.

How do you read this book? Foremost, you can read the book from the beginning to end. You can also pick one page a day for 30 days. Lastly, you can pick any page and let the word on the bottom direct you to a complimentary page and lead you to the next word. Whatever is your method, I hope you enjoy these 30 words and at the end, you will consider building your own list of words that will continue to take your life to new levels of greatness.

Words have power.

Part I

Words that Lift

JOY

Don't postpone joy!

Joy is in the making. Make joy an ongoing process. As each of us has weekly chores - washing, ironing, and cleaning, *joy making* should be listed in that inventory. Creating joy will take you to a place where all dilemmas, problems, bills, concerns, and obstacles fail to exist. If joy is playing the music real loud and dancing naked in the mirror, baby, go on and do it. Play those old 45's on the record player stacked in the back of the closet. Wear mismatched shoes around the house. Bake a cake in a raincoat. Pull out those old picture books and remember those good times. Now, go and make some new joy moments.

I have that saying plastered all over my house. It is my reminder to live in the present. I keep reminding myself that nothing is so great that I should feel low, despondent, or upset. Joy is in my hands! Joy is about this very moment. Real joy celebrates the present!

Although my boss may get on my nerves, the bus may splash me with mud, the kids aren't acting right, the car has a flat tire, and the toaster has burnt the English muffins for the 17th time, joy still abides. It still lingers in my home. What can people do to get joy back in their lives? It is quite simple. Foremost, think about joy. Think about good times. God gave us memories for the purpose of creating joy. In the middle of a snow-covered day in December, remember the joy of a spring day when you played Frisbee with your children or drank lemonade on the front porch or just sat on the stoop watching the cars go by.

Whatever brings you bliss, do it. Whose life is it anyway? Yours. And you deserve joy in it. Life is too short to focus on what couldn't, shouldn't, wouldn't, can't, don't, didn't, and won't. Have you ever met someone who has spent their entire life complaining? How are you today? Oh, my knee is hurting a little. TGIF! Yeah, but I've got so much work to do. They never realize that an aching knee is better than a knee replacement. And having a lot of work to do is better than searching for work as an unemployment statistic. Joy making is healthy. When you embrace joy, you create better thoughts, which in turn create better emotions, which in turn create better feelings, which in turn creates a healthier you.

There are 165 citations to joy in the bible. Nehemiah 8:10 says that *the joy of the Lord is our strength*. Therefore, if you postpone your joy, you postpone your strength. In a world where people feel powerless and spend too much time shopping, eating, watching television, arguing, dieting, and stressing, there must be time for joy. Joy can help, heal, and hurl you into the cosmos as a new human being.

Today, take a moment and Make a *Joy*ful Noise! Bring *Joy* to the World! If you can, bring someone joy! Remember, joy comes from an endless source. There's more than enough to go around. Do some joy work today.

(also read Fun)

FUN

*Rules should always be bent, if not broken.
It's the only way to have any fun.*
— Alyson Noel, *Evermore*

Most of us grew up in neighborhoods where we played games. Game playing taught us social order, social skills, communication, and how to have fun. Fun must be a prerequisite to *having a life!* One of my friends always boasts jokingly about his *Get a Life Campaign*! So few of us have a life and are dependent on our jobs, friends, and family members for sanity. It's unfair to those important people in our lives to be encumbered with your inadequacy to be a whole, productive, and creative individual.

Childhood games are hindering some of us from getting a life and having fun. Freeze Tag, Mother May I, Hide and Seek, Red Light-Green Light are a restrictive part of your life. Who among us are still playing these games, yet not having fun?

Are you playing Freeze tag? Are people able to say things to you and paralyze you, while others say things that free you. Who and why do these people have control over your life?

Are you playing Mother May I? Are parents, siblings, old partners giving you permission to take little itty-bitty steps of progress and then at their whim send you back to the beginning?

Are you playing Hide and Seek? Are you hiding from people who are searching for you? Or are you searching for people who don't want to be found?

Are you playing Red Light-Green Light? Are you allowing persons to stop you in the midst of your stride and keep you frozen until they give you permission to continue? You're always trying to get to the leader, but at their command.

When you believe that life is burdensome, it is! Life gives us what you expect it to: overdue bills, stressful children, uncooperative spouses, unending jobs, nasty clients, long carpools, and fast foods. Life can be a game. There is nothing wrong with playing the game. The problem comes in if you didn't know who and when the rules were made or changed.

I used to have a secretary that had problems every day. Every single thing was a dilemma or the end of the world. If the printer ran out of ink, she ran out of sanity. I thought she was a nut. But I remembered that I was here to have fun and I couldn't change her, but I could change myself. I started breaking stuff in the office. My colleagues said I was being mean. I really was having fun. She eventually stopped the crisis behavior and handled things in a methodical, business-like and expeditious manner. She knew if I touched it in the office, it would break. So, what was there to panic or be grief-stricken about?

Our magic and power come in our ability to make things work for us - make them fun: the disappointments, the hurts, and the games...even the biggest game called Life.

(also read Celebration)

CREATIVITY

Creativity is just connecting things.
- Steve Jobs

I believe each of us was put on this earth to create. Creativity was the first project God set out upon. He toiled hard and long (almost 7,000 years) to make the world with all its living creatures. I know it must have taken God 2000 years just making us. Creativity is the essence of our humanity. Everything you do in the world is based on creativity. You have the creative genius in each of us to even create a sentence that has never been written, heard, or spoken before. Even destruction is based on creativity, the eradication of it. Look around and notice that everything is/was a creative thought of someone.

A movie
A toaster
A book
A computer
A window
A child

As the adage goes, if you create a better mousetrap, they will come. Some people create buildings, paintings, families, and love. Others create war, poverty, chaos, and hate. Creating is the most powerful thing you can do in your lifetime.

    Create a poem.
        Create a character.
            Create a solution.
    Create forgiveness.
        Create a celebration.
            Create a scholarship fund.
    Create a home.
        Create a job for a teenager.
            Create a healthy environment for children.

Create a rock garden.
    Rocks can create pyramids.
        Rocks can create art (Stonehenge).
Art creates inspiration.
    Inspiration creates effort.
        Effort creates ends.

(also read Work)

CELEBRATION

Celebrate what you want to see more of.
— Thomas J. Peters

Some people party their entire lives, but they never celebrate. A celebration can be a party, but not every party is a celebration. A celebration is an event to honor, praise or remember a friend, an event, a place, or an idea.

We don't celebrate enough.

In a world where we overindulge in food, sex, cable, websites, and excuses, take a moment to celebrate. Can you think of all the things that could be celebrated? Let's begin with friendship. My best friend and I celebrated our 5,000th day of knowing each other. We met the first day of high school and have been friends ever since. It was one of the most meaningful days in my life.

Even my alumni friends held a 12-year celebration entitled, *Celebrate Life - Celebrate People* after we lost a classmate. We made a conscious decision to give each member a life tribute while they were here and celebrate the happiness they had brought to each of our lives. Each individual tribute led us to call each other's parents, friends, and partners to find funny anecdotes, high school memories, and childhood dreams. It was a wonderful celebration of people, friendships, and life.

As a society, we have celebrations for events like marriage, divorce, graduation, and birthdays. Why can't we have a celebration to celebrate people just for being themselves - nothing big and unique, just the understanding that each person is special and has made a significant impact to each of our lives. Take a moment and celebrate someone for their uniqueness, ingenuity, divineness, and extraordinary ability to be themselves.

Wouldn't we all love to hear "Here's to you...Hip! Hip! Hooray!"

(also read Let)

FLY

One man can never consent to creep when one feels an impulse to soar.

- Hellen Keller

In many of our dreams and fantasies, we desire to fly. Robert Townsend's movie, *Meteor Man*, had a hilarious scene where he realized he had superpowers, but when he flew he didn't fly any higher than the hood of a car. He was too afraid to get in the clouds.

Flying is hard work. It takes strong wings, the ability to maneuver in strong winds, avoid airplanes and trees, and landing can be the pits. Also, when you are flying you have to be aware of bird hawks, an enemy of small birds.

Many people don't have flying mentalities. Flying gives you a bird's-eye view of the world. Flying means that you are getting there in record time.

That's why I love the song *Fly Like an Eagle*. The words say *I want to fly like an eagle…To the sea. Fly like an eagle. Let my spirit carry me. I want to fly like an eagle… 'Till I'm free.* People like Kweisi Mfume learned how to fly. Colin Powell likes to fly. Joan Rivers, after her life tragedies, still flew. When you allow our situations to weigh us down, it is impossible to get off the ground. If you have broken wings from past relationships, childhood hurts, or emotional trauma, your flying days will never begin. Think light. What will it take you to fly?

In my dreams, I fly around the world. I fly over my problems, through my dilemmas, above my hurts, under my failures, and around my concerns. Flying is one thing that cannot limit me. Even if caged, a bird still can fly within the cage.

When someone asks, how are you today? Tell them *flying high!*

(also read Grace)

CHILDHOOD

It's never too late to have a happy childhood.
                          - Anonymous

Childhoods are like choices. They affect the rest of your life. Childhood is the most pivotal point of your life. Childhood defines, shapes, and outlines our entire life. Your early childhood, school age years, and adolescence build upon your childhood experiences. It is difficult to face that which hurts us. Childhood has hurt many of us, intentionally and coincidentally.

When you realize that the way you do things is a result of our childhood, then you will be able to reorganize, redefine, and restructure your life dramatically. If you make your bed every day it is either because you did that as a child or you didn't do that as a child. When you cannot figure out the little nuances in your life, examine your childhood.

If you attract the wrong mates consistently, examine your childhood. If you are addicted to alcohol, narcotics, sex, television, or food, examine your childhood. If you are afraid of insects, examine your childhood. If you repeat the same patterns of failure, examine your childhood. Each person's childhood was filled with some sort of trauma. Yet, those who are successful, were those who did not make these traumas their playmates, toys, or fears.

How can you improve your childhood and adulthood? You can make childhood better by being a better adult and not bringing into the present those afflictions from childhood. By making a commitment to ensure that at least one child lives a better childhood than yours, is one step to a better adulthood. By partnering with a lover whose childhood is as *traumaless* as possible is another strategy to make a better union and be a better adult.

If you did not have an opportunity to experience childhood wonders, don't deny yourself of those wonders anymore. Your childhood can be repaired, different, even wonderful. If you had *bad* parents, go and adopt some senior citizens and make them your new parents. If you never went to the zoo, go this weekend. If you didn't get the latest toys, take yourself on a toy shopping spree. Create the childhood today that you wanted for yourself from yesterday. You only live once, but childhoods can be repaired and lived again and again!

(also read Thanks)

SUFFICIENCY

Everything that you will ever need, lies within.
 - Susan L. Taylor
   Editor-in-Chief Emerita of *Essence Magazine*

I am sufficient. I am enough. I have what it takes! I am competent, capable, and courageous enough to improve and impact the quality of life of my friends, colleagues, family, and spouse.

I am sufficient.

God pulled together atoms, molecules, proteins, people, nutrients, and 280 days give or take to get me here. I am sufficient. Although mom or dad, boss or subordinate, sibling or friend, may have said that I am not capable, underqualified, overqualified, too old, or too young, I am sufficient. Everything I need to be who I am I have within me.

I am enough for a little child who needs a hug. I am enough for a charity that needs a hand. I am enough for a community that needs help. I am enough for that single mother who needs some hope. I am enough for that senior citizen who needs some happiness. I am sufficient. I am capable of making contributions big or small that can make a difference. I am a sufficient human being: qualified, talented, and able.

There are many millionaires and billionaires who are not sufficient. They help very few people, give to very less, and hide from so many. They live lives that destroy, rather than ones that build people and their dreams.

Sufficient people put their resources (time, talent, and money) into people, their dreams and their future, and not into corporations, companies, and stocks.

I am sufficient. I am worthy of someone to love me passionately, respectfully, and thoroughly.

I am sufficient.

Thoughts of doubt, despair, and doom are lies told to me by people, circumstances, and past experiences.

I am sufficient.

Although I may have not received the promotion or raise, sustained a great marriage, or raised a successful family, I am still enough. I am sufficient. I am sufficient because time allows me to try again. I can correct those things that I have blundered, apologize to those I have hurt, untie the knots I have made, get off at the next exit for the one that went by, take another shot for the one that I missed, and exit and reboot the system that has stalled or crashed. I have time, chances, and resources at my disposal. Don't tell me what I am not. Tell me what I am.

I am sufficient!

(also read Giving)

FAITH

Faith is knowing that if I step out in the darkness, there will be something to stand upon or I will be taught how to fly.
                             - Iyanla Vanzant

Memory is a unique part of our makeup as human beings. We rely upon it to navigate our way through life. By remembering numbers, addresses, directions, names, and memories, it constructs the very essence of our humanity. Memories help us decipher those things that may be harmful, helpful, or honest. People who possess better memories usually do better academically, socially, and vocationally.

Faith and memory are interrelated. There are three types of memory: short-term, long-term, and remote. Short-term memory refers to working memory that stays around only for a few moments between 15 - 30 seconds. For example, someone tells you their phone number. If you don't transfer it mentally to your long-term memory, then it's gone. Long-term memory involves our ability to recognize childhood places, work routines, friends, family, and foes. Remote memory encompasses still knowing how to ride a bike after five years of never riding one, speaking, reading, brushing your teeth, and combing your hair. These are deeply ingrained memories that are rarely lost even after severe illnesses. Remote memories can withstand a lot, but why does our faith withstand so little?

Here's how memory and faith should be interrelated. Your faith should be like a remote memory: deeply ingrained. Your response to chaotic, catastrophic, and calamitous events should be a remote spiritual memory, kicking in as strong as your ability and knowledge of speaking. God has shown up for you in times of crisis. So the very moment when your car won't start, why does our temporary, short-term, and long-term memory fail you and you forget that God will provide. When the doctor tells you that your cancer has returned, does your faith fail? As you remember how to walk, by placing one foot in front of the other, your faith should kick in, with unwavering measure in times of doubt and despair. A faithful response almost has to mirror a biological response. Innate. Resolute. Natural. Kicking in anytime your natural order is threatened.

We cannot continue to evict faith. Two forces cannot occupy the same space at the same time. Fear eliminates faith and doubt counts faith out.   Some tests are just that - tests of faith. How will you respond? Will you fall to pieces or will you stand with your faith, knowing that the devil has a limitation on what he can do. Faith is a foundational part of spirituality. It undergirds your relationship with God and strengthens your walk in life.

Faith is not just saying; it is doing. So be faithful. Walk, breathe, and live knowing that God is there and will respond at your greatest time of need. It pleases God to come to your rescue, to work a miracle on your behalf, and to defeat evil time and time again! Faith will see you through!

(also read God)

MIRACLE

I am realistic – I expect miracles.
           - Wayne W. Dyer

It is easy to talk about miracles. Growing up, many of us read about Jesus being born to a virgin or Jesus walking on water. There are even miracles on the nightly news. A little girl who was stuck in a well is saved. A little boy is found alive after a week under a crumbling building. Miracles are daily experiences in our lives. But how many of us have really experienced a miracle - One where we saw it unfold in front of our eyes.

In 1998, a miracle happened in my life. Miracles aren't always big and dramatic. Sometimes they can be the smallest thing. Rev. Dr. Renita Weems, Biblical Scholar and ordained elder says, "A miracle is simply defined by timeliness." It probably can be explained scientifically, but does that count it out as a miracle? Absolutely not! If you are in dire need of something and are in your last moment to receive it and it arrives...isn't that a miracle? I think it is.

So here I was on May 4, 1998 arguing with the Dean of the Graduate School about the problems with my dissertation. My advisor is by my side defending me and my 150 or so page document. Then the dean slipped up and cursed at both of us. My advisor stood up and said, "I don't have to put up with this!" Slammed the door. And left me there to defend my paper, myself, and the 25 years of my life I had put into this educational pursuit. And I did. I sat there for the next 3 hours and went point for point on his corrections, questions, and advice. Finally, I looked him in the eyes and said, "If you want to fight, we can fight. I can get a lawyer, the newspapers, the TV stations and we can fight it out!" The Dean knew I wasn't playing and said, "Well, you can have your second meeting, but I will have problems to get your committee together in the next 10 minutes." I needed a miracle to pull this meeting off.

To graduate from the institution, every student had to hold three meetings, otherwise known as verbal defenses. Most institutions only have 2, but this one had three. All grades were due in the registrar's office on May 5 and the only hope I had was to conduct meeting #2 today and the final meeting tomorrow on May 5th. I needed a miracle.

When I stood to leave his office, it was 10 minutes until 2 p.m. My colloquium started in ten minutes at 2 p.m. and I had to find all three of my committee members. I ran and found my advisor and one of my other committee members. But my third member was at lunch. The Dean was ready to go, but my third member was missing. Ten minutes passed. Then another ten minutes passed. Then another ten minutes passed, and my third member was nowhere to be found. The dean entered the conference room and announced that I would have to cancel my colloquium because my entire committee was not present. At that moment, the secretary entered the room and announced that my third committee member was on the phone and was on his way.

I took a sigh of relief; the dean made a sigh of disgust. I began my presentation upon my committee member's arrival. I knew the subject matter. I explained the statistical procedure called discriminant analysis and the coefficient of determination like I can explain how to make lemonade. I was in my zone. At the end of my presentation, my committee asked questions, then the dean chimed in with a question that seemed utterly ridiculous. My third committee member said, "It looks very simple to me...don't you see it?" That silenced the dean for the remainder of the presentation. They asked me to leave the room. And my advisor knew that if I didn't get on the schedule for the next morning, I wouldn't be graduating. I needed a miracle.

So I sat in the lobby praying and the secretary began to talk to me and tell me that everything will be okay. She went on to talk about how God had worked a miracle in her life this week when she received an insurance refund which helped her pay an outstanding bill. I told her that was a miracle. Then the door opens and my advisor puts her thumb up. I knew I was scheduled for the next day. I walked into the room and each of my committee members stood up. My advisor looked at me and said, "Congratulations Dr. Davis!"

There was my miracle and I became the first student to never have to conduct an oral defense in the university's history. I have continued to look for miracles daily, whether large or small, timed or untimed.

(also read Power)

GOD

(A little boy looks to heaven and says...)
God, you never got back to me about that lamp I broke.

It is God, in whom we trust. God is an entity, deity, or being. The more God and I communicate, the more I am amazed at his diversity. The song that says He's the same yesterday, today, and forever more is a cliché'. God is changing everyday as each of us do. He is a dynamic God! He is a metamorphic God. He has to be to deal with human beings like myself and that has to be a difficult, if not, a daunting task. Humans can be so inconsistent, fickle, and spurious. At other times, we can be so giving, kind, nurturing, great, and triumphant. What fascinates me is that God possesses some of these same characteristics that we demonstrate. Remember, we were made in His image.

When Adam and Eve didn't follow his directions, not only did he punish the snake (neighbor's child), but he put Adam and Eve out. I can see many of our parents who have had enough of a grown child and put him/her out. Later on, in a fit of anger, God just kills 10,000 people. It seems God needed some anger management classes. For God couldn't figure out why it was so difficult for the human being (His creation) to do what he said do. Then he became one. He came down as Christ and realized that life was a difficult thing. God didn't have it any easier either. He was persecuted, spat upon, falsely accused, then killed by the very people He created.

How is it that God struggled in humanity? Isn't he God, the creator and master of all things? I am able to talk about God because of our relationship. I always remind people that God and I are on a first-name basis. Our relationship is one of give and take. This relationship isn't a dictatorship, not autocratic. Relationship building is about give and take. For God to understand his creation, God had to become human to understand humanity.

So when God went back to heaven, He became like a grandparent: understanding, patient, and empathetic. God understands our plight now because of his journey through Christ. After his journey, God is no longer quick to anger. Yet you are still working on yours. In his realm of perfection, God has developed into what each of strives to become: better. Yes, God has become better. He is more kind with his creation, more patient, still loving, yet understanding, with grace, and a level of forgiveness that is needed. He's just God in His awesome wonder.

Try to understand God more by understanding others. Serve God better by serving others. Please God by living a victorious life. Love God more by loving those who persecute you. Live in God by being better! Strengthen your relationship with God by improving your relationship skills of communication, trust, humility, and compromise.

You serve a mighty God, a God that becomes more and more perfect.

(also read Help)

PART II

Words that Yield

HELP

*Ask for help not because you are weak,
but because you want to remain strong.*
- Les Brown

Why are our egos so large and fragile that we will sit powerless instead of asking for help? Help! Scream it from the rooftops, under the bridge, inside the burning car, while enduring your failing relationship, staring at your blinking TV - Help! Don't be embarrassed; it can be a natural response. Help indicates that we are an interdependent society. We are connected on many levels, but primarily on a level to give and receive help from each other.

Help! Let the world know you need it, and the world will provide it. It is a part of our human makeup to help people, animals, and *misspelled* words. Help! I hear you ready to yell it. Help! It is not sign of weakness, nor anguish, nor ignorance. It tells the world your sense of urgency and respect for others who have the necessary skills, knowledge, and abilities to get you out of the jam that you may be in, the jam you're getting out of, or the one you may be heading into.

Help! Have you screamed it yet? If or when you scream help, make sure you scream it at the right time. Screaming help in an abandoned building can be risky. No one may be there to come. Screaming help in a plane going down is a futile response. You must scream help at the right time, place, and situation. Don't scream recklessly. I promise help will arrive. Scream help in a room of geniuses. Scream help at the therapist's office. Scream help to your children in reference to the new electronic gadgets that have you dumbstruck. Shout it! Yell it! Wail it! Cry it!

Indicating you need help usually gets people moving. There's a need for human beings to come to the rescue! When you yell help, the universe must respond. You are here as co-creators of the universe and our God. Why wouldn't he send help? It is in his divine makeup to give us what you need. Help is one of the many things that He provides.

Asking for help is a strategic tool. The ask is an intentional request for resources. The ask indicates to the world I need support that I cannot find, don't have the energy to act upon nor the emotional capacity to take another step. As you use a hammer to a nail, asking for help activates the world around you. Just like turning on a switch, I don't know how it works, but I know the lights come on.

The helpers of the world are the least paid, but some of the happiest people alive. They thrive on giving assistance to those who really need it. Yet, a large percentage of clients are resistant to help or to change. So when people come forth asking for help and are willing to accept it, it pleases the helping community.

I love going to the library and seeing the joy a librarian gets when they help you solve a complex research question or find the right journal or the right fact.

When you yell help, help is on the way.

(also read Life)

FORGIVENESS

Forgiveness is the fragrance that the violet sheds on the heel that has crushed it.
— Mark Twain

When we forgive, we give. We give away those weights that are keeping us down. We give away insecurities. We give away childhood traumas, adolescent nightmares, and adult dooms. Holding onto hurts, pains, and grudges is toxic, unhealthy and defeating.

One of the hardest things to do in life is to forgive someone who has hurt you. It can be a humbling experience and a healing one. People usually cannot see the healing side of forgiveness. Forgiveness is a state of vulnerability. It is the ability to place your life in the same situation, trusting the same person will not take advantage of you again. When you can do that, then you really know that you have forgiven them.

Forgiveness is not about being stupid. It has a lot to do with trust and growth. Once you can trust again, you can grow. You can move forward. We are a society of blame. We make other people accountable for the hurts and disappointments others have inflicted upon us. Will you forgive what momma said, or where papa touched you, or what sister took from you, or the friend that ruined your marriage? Forgiveness is a prerequisite for greatness.

Forgive and forget is one of the ludicrous clichés of our time. No one forgets, nor should you. If you forget how to cross the street, your chances of being run over increase. Who said you should forget and why? Remembering certain instances gives us the wisdom, mother wit and intelligence that you learn through experience. It heightens your intuition, perception, and insight. Experience is a type of learning method, just like auditory, kinetic, or visual.

Make forgiveness an internal behavior. Know that each time you forgive it cleanses, releases, and revitalizes your spirit from these dissenting memories. The more you forgive, the healthier you become.

Forgive...

Start forgiving and give it away.

(also read Forgiveness....read it again!)

GIVING

We do not make a living by what we get.
We make a life by what we give.
          - Winston Churchill

When we think of giving, we often think of the Holiday season, birthdays, and celebrations. We think of chestnuts, snow, Santa, reindeers, cake, balloons, presents and children all aglow.

The September 11th bombings, the continuous mass shootings, the 2020 riots have created a nation that is in desperate need of each other. Those horrific days have shortened the degrees of separation for every American. Somehow and somewhere, we were connected to these tragedies…whether we knew someone, or it impacted our emotional well-being.

And our response as a nation was to give. And it was admirable and wondrous that we gave money for families who lost children, lovers, husbands, wives, aunts, and grandparents. We gave millions! Yet, my hope and charge are also that we will give what is needed when that widow is sitting alone during Christmas. We have to intercede for those who may begin to lose faith and hope. We have to keep reminding those persons that things will get better. We have to remind them that each of us will make it and will find the ultimate good and greatness that God has deemed for us to survive from this event or any tragedy.

Our challenge is to keep giving, but not only from our economic coffers, but to people and projects that will provide clarity, hope, redemption, insight, goodness and truth. Let's give an ear to each other. Give an extra moment of your day before you hustle on to your life. Exchange a smile at the person at the counter. Buy a stranger a cup of coffee.

And whatever you do, keep giving love. Love each other until every heart is healed, every horrible memory is minimized, each faithless person begins to embrace the belief that God is alive because of our example. You can be a world that gives until you reach the threshold of peace across the world.

It is your reasonable service to be givers.

(also read Selflessness)

COMMITMENT

Unless commitment is made, there are only promises and hopes, but no plans.
- Peter F. Drucker

A commitment is like a stamp. You need to stick to it until you get somewhere. Geniuses are merely people who commit to something for a lifetime without looking for rewards, praise, or acknowledgment. They just keep working at it until someone says, "Wow!" Even then, many of these geniuses don't want to hear your comments. They simply go back to their genius residency.

Spiritual Commitments

I will start the morning off without confusion, noise, and chaos. I will meditate at least one minute in the morning before I leave the house getting in tune with myself, my energies, my God. I will pray to the one who knows me best. I will read at least one scripture a day. I will reflect on my day and be courageous enough to admit the problems of the day that I caused.

Physical Commitments

I will begin a diet that is healthy, fat-reduced, fiber increased, fruit, vegetable, and water laden. I will take the steps at least twice a week instead of taking the elevator. Find a workout partner to keep each other motivated. Ask your doctor if you are the ideal weight and work on becoming that. Take care of your skin. Invest in a pedicure. Exercise vigorously weekly, walk moderately daily and sleep deeply nightly.

Emotional Commitments

Start making a commitment to build, nurture, and sustain familial relationships. Forgive those who have hurt you. Forgive yourself for those who you have hurt. Be aware of your emotions. Your emotions should not dictate how your day goes, how you respond to colleagues, and how you feel. If your emotions control you, instead of you controlling your emotions, then you should consider seeing a professional. You are the masters of your moods, emotions, and desires. Stop laughing when things aren't funny and crying when things aren't sad.

Financial Commitments

Commit to be as debt-free as possible. Commit to placing aside 10% of your salary. Even if you can't afford to putting aside 10%, start with 5%, start with 2%, but start. Then keep increasing the amount that you put aside. Make a financial commitment to give consistently to some charity or program. At least once a year, cash your paycheck. Look at the money and then deposit it again. Look at your worth in real cash. If you are not satisfied with what you see, commit to improvement.

If you want to see an aspect of your life improve, commit!

(also read Covenant)

WORK

Choose a job you love, and you will never have to work a day in your life.
— Confucius

The bible tells us clearly that God worked for 6 days and rested on the seventh. Whoever created the work week, I'm glad they didn't take God's suggestion and make it a 6-day work week. I think many of us would have died. We are a society that works. Our economy is reliant upon the purchase and sale of labor. Our economy works its best when unemployment is at least 5%. Since there will never be enough jobs available for the people who are looking, work becomes a position of stature.

Human beings work on a variety of things. We work overtime. We work on building our careers. We work on our cars, homes, and our backyards. We work on our bodies by spending an inordinate amount of time in the gym. We work and work and work. But rarely do we work on our humanity.

We are the only species that kills unnecessarily. We are the only species that kills and brings extinction to other species. We are the only species that destroys the world in which we inhabit. We are the only species that creates dysfunctional children with our words, actions, and behaviors. We are the only species that likes to see each other suffer.

On the other hand, the human race has brilliance pumping through its veins. We are the only species that creates beautiful cities, magnificent cathedrals, and breath-taking paintings. We write poetry to soothe, music to heal, and literature to help. We are the only species that creates foods to slay our taste buds, literature to kidnap us away from reality and technology to improve our lives. We are the only species that knows how to get the most out of a dollar at a bargain sale.

If we do so many things well, why can't we work on our humanity until it becomes a masterpiece? There is nothing harder than working on yourself. Insecurities, hang-ups, emotional dilemmas, childhood traumas, adult traumas, failed relationships, lost loves, broken hearts, misunderstood purposes, compassion, commitment, accountability, and communication are just some of the many experiences and traits that we must master.

We need a humanity promotion. There are too many of us employed in entry level positions of: complainers, miserables, hopeless, despondents, bullies, crybabies, pity partiers, no focusers, pessimists, doubters, paranoids, cheaters, whiners, exhibitionists, opportunists, and straight up fakes!

Our human race is in need of some executives, CEO's, and entrepreneurs: visionaries, advocates, intercessors, speakers (who will speak up in time of crisis), doers, followers, leaders, completers (who will get the job done), fixers (someone who will come in and fix where the holes in our thinking, our structure, our future), protectors (who will protect those who are the most vulnerable), and gods (who will create, listen, solve, and be gracious) to all.

Start working on your humanity...there's a job opening...your community is interviewing.

(also read Life)

POWER

*Power concedes nothing without a demand!
It never did and it never will!*
                              - Frederick Douglass

Power is the main reason we have work, family, and relationship problems. People who are trying to get power, wield power, yield power, or shield power are usually the problem makers among us. Research indicates that there are 7 types of power: legitimate, reward, coercive, connection, personal, expert, and referent. These power models are used daily in board rooms of corporate America and on the sandlots of kindergarten recess. Power is innate. We like to charge and be in charge. I bet if I asked what percentage of your supervisors were great, many of the responses would be less than 40%. Why is this? Power is abused, misused, and confused.

Seven ways to use power more effectively is by mastering these:

Legitimate Power is the power that comes with the position that you hold. There are powerful positions that you can get your bang for your buck and really impact the world. Mentor, Friend, Parent, Lover, Listener, Cook, ... Find a position that does not stress, but strengthens.

Reward Power is the power that comes with providing rewards. Random acts of kindness

Coercive Power is denying or offering rewards and firing, or suspending someone.

Connection Power is the power that comes with being connected to top leaders or organizations.

Personal Power is the power you as an individual can generate.

Expert Power is the power that comes when one has access to key knowledge, information, and skills.

Referent Power is the power that comes with the ability to relate to fellow workers which includes being liked and having commitment from followers.

While there are many who have power, there are others who use it to make others feel powerless. The ultimate goal and responsibility of power is to empower those who are hopeless. Power has taken down kings and queens, presidents and CEOs, friends and foes. Use power in a context that is helpful, uplifting, and life changing. Wield power today for the good of someone else!

(also read Miracle)

SEVEN

And on the seventh day God ended his work which he had made; and he rested on the seventh day from all his work which he had made. And God blessed the seventh day, and sanctified it: because that in it he had rested from all his work which God created and made.
- Genesis 2:2-3

Seven represents completion and perfection. Throughout the Bible, seven is used as a metaphor for completion. In Christian teachings, there are seven deadly sins and seven heavenly virtues. There are seven gifts of the Holy Spirit. The Jewish Menorah has seven candles. In the Koran, they speak about seven heavens and walking around the Kabba in Mecca seven times. In Islam, there are seven heavens and seven hells. In Buddhism, the baby Buddha rises and takes seven steps. Hinduism speaks about seven higher worlds and seven underworlds. In Japanese mythology, there are seven gods of good fortune.

For travelers, there are seven wonders of the world. For gamblers, seven is represented as a jackpot and good luck. There are seven colors in the rainbow. There are seven oceans, seven continents, seven notes, seven games in playoffs for Hockey, Baseball and Basketball. There are even seven holes in your head.

To that end, I utilize seven in my life. If God worked six days and rested the seventh, was that a coincidence or god-ordained strategy? Jericho's walls came tumbling down after they walked around seven times. Was that a coincidence or god-ordained strategy? Jacob worked for Rachel's hand in marriage for seven years. There were seven tribes of Judah. Delilah cut off Sampson's seven locks of hair. Jesus uttered seven last words on the cross. Our week is made up of seven days. Our year is made up of 52 weeks. $5 + 2 = 7$

Seven is a God-ordained number. Seven is utilized throughout history in critical points. It sustains the most vital parts of the Bible and is one of the first numbers God uses in Genesis. Start being aware of where seven enters your life. Embrace it! If God did, why not you?

You have seven days a week to make your life one of greatness. When I coach newly laid off people, I lay out a seven-day formula for each day. I tell them on Monday and Tuesday to scour the databases, webpages, and their personal sources for job leads. On Wednesday, prepare application materials for those leads and get them out. On Thursday, treat yourself for accomplishing Monday – Wednesday. On Friday, call a friend and get grounded that this too shall pass. On Saturday, get out of the house and do something that requires you to enjoy nature. On Sunday, rest, eat well, laugh, encourage yourself and focus on the next week and if you are called for an interview, prepare for the upcoming interview. Start over on Monday. This seven-day formula has worked and taken the insanity out of job hunting.

What seven-day strategy could you begin to improve your life? What seven-day strategy could you implement that will move your life forward, little by little, one day at a time, until you reach greatness?

(also read Death)

RISK

People who live life in fear of taking risks die without living it.
— Fola, *The Seed*

I moved three times in one year. I became a landlord. I lived in Las Vegas, Baltimore, and Hyattsville all in one year. I gave my two dogs away. I started two new jobs. I drove 2600 miles by myself in 4 days.

It was a year of risks. Calculated risks are the best ways to achieve. Moving 2600 miles away to Nevada, I was exposed to the concept of wealth building, entrepreneurship, and investing. I even conquered my fear of falling asleep after 3 hours of driving. In fact, I drove 16 hours in one day straight from Memphis to Baltimore. God was with me! I took risks!

No one can be successful without factoring, embracing, and measuring risks. Throughout the Bible, God took risks. Just by giving us freewill, God risked. Eve and Adam took a risk. Noah took a risk. Jesus even risked it all. The concept of faith is risk: risking to believe in a religion that will get you to heaven. Risks are healthy and move us out of our comfort zone and can lead us to a road of greatness. Examine your life. Examine your failures. Examine your greatest moments. Then risk living again!

Why do we take risks? Foremost, we take risks to change our situation. Mediocrity is a disease and all diseases eventually kill you! If you are fed up with your relationships, your job, or your financial status in life, only risks bring about a change. The same behavior yields the same results. So risk something! Risk renewing your marriage or a friendship. Risk updating some work-related skills. Risk opening an investment account.

We risk in order to grow. We are here to grow and not just suffer. Growth is a part of the human experience. Risking helps us stretch our boundaries, test our faith, and use skills and resources we never knew existed.

Lastly, we risk in order to end up in our ultimate place of victory. All calculated risks will bring you to where you are ultimately supposed to be. It was funny that for two years I looked for a job in the D.C. area. I went on interviews. I landed a few second interviews and knew that I had the job. But somehow I didn't get them. The jobs didn't come through... the budgets were restricted... hiring freezes were put in place. So I took a risk and accepted a job 2600 miles away to only end up four blocks from D.C. six months later. Isn't God faithful for those who take risks?

Take a moment and examine your life, your situations, and your future and make a decision to risk something in order to get something. Your destiny is waiting!

(also read End)

SLAVERY

Slavery is stupid because you own no one but yourself.

by Mr. Greenberg's 4th Grade Class
January 1998

You may be surprised to see slavery as one of the 30 words. From 1619 to 1863, slavery was perhaps one of the most arduous times in our nation's history. The ramifications on generations of families should remind us that we can do better as a nation. We are still haunted by nightmares of this history because we can't make peace with this past.

Slavery comes in different forms. There are institutions perpetuating slavery in this day and age. A bank who charges you 29% to use their credit card, gives you less than 1% on your savings account, and denies you a home loan is a slavery institution. Educational facilities that allow students and teachers to arrive late, teach little and leave early is a slave institution. Churches that collect offerings for first ladies, pastoral anniversaries, vacations, and car funds and do not support the community at the same financial level is a slave holder. Retail stores that increase prices to put them back on sale at the original prices are slave institutions. Friends who allow you to remain the same mediocre, average, boring person are helping you to remain enslaved. Families that allow generational addictions, sufferings, and wounds to persist are slave holders. Slavery, in all forms, must meet resistance, rebellion, and retaliation.

Take example from great figures in this era. Be a Harriet Tubman - Go back in your community and free someone. Someone is waiting for you to return. They may not have the courage, understanding, or vision to attain their own freedom. They may need you to assist them.

Be an Olado Equiano...expose your slave holders to the world. Join a civic or political organization that is dedicated to exposing the social, racial, and economic injustices in the world. If we want to repeat slavery or the Holocaust or the Jim Jones murder, all we have to do is say and do nothing. Evil has a way of returning again and again.

Let us learn from slaves who refused to be enslaved by rebelling or becoming runaways. Rebel against addiction, debt, physical and verbal abuse. Run away from emotional, spiritual, mental and sexual molestation.

If you are in slavery, purchase your freedom. Freedom can be purchased through education, economic development (start a business), or by giving your time and talent to those organizations and institutions that show an interest in developing your community, your children, and your cause.

Slavery in any form is deplorable. Will you choose to be free or enslaved?

(also read Freedom)

CHOICES

Every person has free choice. Free to obey or disobey the Natural Laws. Your choice determines the consequences. Nobody ever did, or ever will, escape the consequences of his choices.

- Alfred A. Montapert

All of us have choices to make. Whether it is to fly or freeze, sing or shout, run or walk, or live or thrive, we have choices to make.

The consequences of making choices should be one of the first lessons parents teach their children. Choosing to put your hand on a hot stove results in a burn. Choosing to not look both ways when crossing the street can result in a pedestrian accident or worse, death. Children and adults need a thorough understanding that the choices one has made in one's life will lead them to the place and position they are today.

Choices can haunt us. Bad choices can pick at us and torture us throughout a lifetime. Horrible choices can keep our lives at a level of despair and disaster. Good choices can free us from ourselves. And better choices can make our lives soar to immeasurable heights.

If you have a life of making bad choices, then get a CHOICES BOARD. What is a CHOICES BOARD? A Choices Board is a group of your closest three to five friends that will sit on your Board and help make choices with you. When the decisions are essential, you present these decisions to your CHOICES BOARD who will call an executive meeting and return with a final recommendation for you to accept or decline.

As the adage goes, "what one does today affects the rest of your life." The greatest lesson you can teach a child is how to make wise and useful choices. Their life will depend on it.

(also read Change)

PART III

Words that Free

LET

Let freedom ring!

- Martin Luther King, Jr.

To give permission or opportunity...allow...used to express a command, request, or proposal....To release from ....to come down gradually; lower....

Let has a multitude of definitions. It is a phenomenal verb, because it calls things into being. Things happen when one uses the word let. Let announces to the world that I'm about to work on some things. God's first utterance was Let. God commanded - *Let there be light*.

Throughout the entire creational story in Genesis, God uses the word let. If you read just the first chapter of Genesis, let is used ten times. Light came into existence when God said Let. The sky was created when God said Let. The land appeared when God said Let. The grass sprouted when God said Let. Stars twinkled in the sky above when God said Let. Living creatures like the fish, birds, and cattle where actualized with the little word, Let. Even Man was contrived by God with the word Let. Human beings were given the law of the land when God said, "Let man have dominion over all living things." Therefore, let is a creational word.

If you believe you have the ability to create goodness, greatness, and genius, begin using the word let. Too many of us need to "Let go of it!" If you get stuck in the past, "Let's move on." Mark Twain wrote, "Let us so live that even when we die even the undertaker will be sorry."

Jesus said, "Let the little children come unto me." Preachers preach, "Let go and let God!" Daily, "Let us fix our eyes on Jesus, the author and perfecter of our faith, who for the joy set before him endured the cross, scorning its shame, and sat down at the right hand of the throne of God." -Hebrew 12:2

Let this be a blessed day.
Let me experience joy.
Let there be peace.
Let us celebrate each other.
Let me be a blessing to someone today.
Let us break bread together.
Let's make a joyful noise unto the Lord.
Let goodness and mercy follow me all the days of my life.
Let my enemies stumble and fall.
Let it be.

(also read Time)

TIME

Some people are controlled by others.
Some people are controlled by no one.
But all of us are controlled by time.

If you knew exactly when you would die, the question is not what you would do differently. The question is what you would do. The story of the little clock demonstrates what you must do.

There was a little clock that sat on the shelf. This clock sat next to the grandfather clock. And the little clock had to tick and tock, tick and tock, tick and tock...31,536,000 times a year. It had to tick and tock and tick and tock and then one day the little clock said, "Look! I can't do this! I can't tick and tock 31,536,000 times year."

Then the grandfather clock came over to the little clock and said, "Little clock, you don't have to worry about a tick and a tock and a tick and a tock. All you have to do little clock is tick. And tock! And tick! And tock! And tick! And tock! But make sure, little clock...that each one of your ticks and each one of your tocks......counts!"

Time makes all of us equal, no matter how rich, beautiful, tall, short, or thin we are. We have been equally distributed time. Each year, each of us has 31,536,000 seconds. It's up to us to use it wisely or waste it foolishly. Let us live each day as if the end of the day was our last. In essence, it is. We have lost those valuable seconds. Have we made them count or have we just counted them?

The greatest predictor of your potential is how you spend your time. Do you spend it studying, networking, and developing? Or do you spend it couching, gossiping, and procrastinating? None of us can say that we were treated unfairly by time. Time is the fairest of all equal opportunities.

(also read Let)

GRACE

"What is grace? It is the inspiration from on high: it is love; it is liberty. Grace is the spirit of law. This discovery of the spirit of law belongs to Saint Paul; and what he calls "grace" from a heavenly point of view, we, from an earthly point, call "righteousness.

- Victor Hugo

(the state of being protected or blessed by the favor of God)

It is grace that woke us up this morning. It is grace that deals with us so gently and doesn't take us out of here. It is grace that understands our shortcomings and blesses us anyhow. Grace will do that.

Grace is the product that is created from the love affair that God has with us. God, not only loves us, He is in love with us. He adores us, admires us, chastises us, and tries to build a relationship that is deeper and more meaningful. Many of us run and hide from God. While others don't even realize that there is someone in love with them deeply. He thinks about us night and day. He isn't selfish nor stubborn nor inconsiderate. He gives us everything we need! Grace will do that.

Even when we ignore our relationship with God, grace steps in during the interim. Grace protects our relationship and fixes the holes that are created because of our relationship neglect with our maker. Grace will do that.

Grace is not impacted by our lack of care, our inconsistent behaviors, our selfishness, and our phoniness. Grace still loves us and guides us through this life in a blessed manner. Grace will do that.

Any day that you successfully make it to work and home safely, Grace was there. If you fly from point A to point B and there's not a problem with your flight, Grace was there. If your children have been protected from childhood diseases, neighborhood violence, and societal vices, Grace was there. If you survived layoffs, downsizing, rightsizing and the like, Grace was there!

Grace is there to usher you through those difficult times of life. When you know this concept of grace, your rough times don't last as long. Learn to lean on Grace. Be confident that Grace's main purpose is to show up, protect you and shield you, whether you deserve it or not.

Grace will do that!

(also read Seven)

THANKS

In everything, give thanks...
- 1 Thessalonians 5:18

They are two simple words, but mean so much to others: Thank you. These words are engraved in my vocabulary… in my every day journey. I use them endlessly now because I remember the days when I barely would. One Sunday following a church service, I left my church with a few friends of mine, including the Pastor. The pastor held the door for everyone to exit. As I was the last one, he looked at me and all of my friends and said, "Not one of you said thank you." I was embarrassed at how I took for granted someone even holding a door open for me. And if I did that, I know I had taken others for granted for even greater things.

So from this day forth, I began to incorporate thank you into my daily locutions.

Whenever I ask someone to do something at work, whether it is their job or not, I say thank you.

When I get let over in traffic, I raise my hand to acknowledge the driver… I say thank you.

Whenever I receive a gift or a compliment, I say thank you.

Thank you is more than an automatic response; it says that I recognize, appreciate, and am grateful for your actions, words, and deeds.

Thank your spouse for loving you. Thank your parents for raising you (good or bad). Thank your children for bringing you heartache and joy. Thank your friends for years of memories. Thank your pastor for helping your spiritual path stay narrow.

Thank you must be a daily part of our language to yourself and to others.

(also read Childhood)

EDUCATION

If you are planning for a year, sow rice; if you are planning for a decade, plant trees; if you are planning for a lifetime, educate people.
- *Chinese Proverb*

There are a lot of things in life that the world can take from you. I never really understood this until a student came into my office and said, "Mr. Davis, I need..." I corrected them in an instant and I said, "Dr. Davis!" Their face showed anguish and irritation. The student said, "Well, what is the difference?" And I had to ponder. I didn't really know. I had worked hard, but I didn't feel any smarter. I wrote the dissertation, but I didn't feel any greater. I impressed my dissertation committee, but I didn't feel any more gifted. I had just changed the M in Mr. to a D!

Then it hit me. There was a difference. Now, it was not the obvious difference that many of the pompous scholars at universities will tell you. It wasn't that I could handle the rigor or that I understood the coefficient of determination as a statistical procedure. Nor was it that I knew my dissertation so well I could explain it to a little child. The answer came when a credit card company called me to collect a three-month back payment. I had been so involved in my dissertation that I forgot to pay any bills. The electric company called and threatened to disconnect the power. The bank called and told me that I was behind on my car payments. I had all of this money in the bank and hadn't stopped to pay a thing.

And I told this credit card lady (why are they always so combative?) that you can take everything from me...my home, my car, my credit, but you cannot take my education. In a few days, I will be Dr. Roger W. Davis. I may be homeless or living in a dark house, but I will still be Dr. Davis - silence on the other end of the phone.

Education cannot be returned. It is a non-refundable item. It rarely becomes a sale item, but it was one of the most valuable items in life's store. Don't expect a cashier to ring it up. You are responsible for ringing up this item, packaging it, and bringing it home. No one really understands an education's value except your destiny. Education is a luxury item. It can shape a human being into a dreamer or a doer. Education is not primarily about an occupation, as much as about an opportunity. Educators need to stop telling young people to go to school to become a lawyer or a doctor or a this or a that. Go get an education so you can create opportunities for yourself and other people.

Education is a freeing experience. Educate yourself and get the shackles off of your life.

(also read Work)

FREEDOM

The willingness to sacrifice is the prelude to freedom.
- Pesach Seder

Purchase it. Seize it. Plead for it. Wait for it. Whatever you do, get to freedom.

Beloved, the Pulitzer Prize winning book by Toni Morrison and movie produced by Oprah Winfrey is a wonderful example of freedom. Margaret Garner, the main character, kills her children instead of having them enslaved. In Oprah Winfrey's adaption of the movie, there is a scene where she talks about her 28 days of freedom. Her character, Sethe, had escaped from the plantation and was free for 28 days before they came to take her children. But in essence, she really wasn't free. She was simply safe for those 28 days and had to always look over her shoulder for her slave owner to return.

Very few of us are free, including myself. Someone owns us if we are always looking over our shoulder because of debts, desires, disasters, and dismay. Richard N. Dixon, a prominent African American and past Treasurer for the State of Maryland, indicated in a speech that he was a free man. He was an elected official, wealthy, and had the ability to retire tomorrow and live a very comfortable life. Freedom lies in what actually is your possession. That's why I like and encourage education. No one can take it from you. They can foreclose on my house, repossess my car, auction my belongings, but they can't take my degrees. I may be homeless, broke, and walking, but I'm still an educated man.

It saddens and shocks me to go to the tax sale each year and see homes that had been completely paid off auctioned for a few thousand dollars in back taxes. You must begin to live your life in a manner that requires you to free yourself. Diminish credit. Live within our means. Terminate dead relationships.

Fire negative friends. Work at a place you love. Live a life that is nourishing.

Stop looking over your shoulder. If you are doing this, you know that the Master will eventually come and get you. Whether the Master is debt, a skeleton in your closet, or a lie on a resume, the Master will come! Take the steps necessary to be a free person.

No matter how you obtain it, freedom must be your end result. Let us understand that freedom is a lonely place. What are you willing to lose, sacrifice, or take on in order to be free? This is the critical question you must ask yourself each day you stay enslaved?

What is this sacrifice? Specifically, what is it for you?

(also read Education)

COVENANT

A covenant made with God should be regarded not as restrictive but as protective.
— Russell M. Nelson

Some gay friends of mine were having a commitment ceremony and asked me to write something special for them. I agreed and began researching biblically and historically things that would be appropriate. They, like myself, didn't believe in *gay marriage* not because of its equal status, but because marriage is not the greatest institution to emulate with estimates declaring that 50%+ of marriages end in divorce. The best model I found for my friends was the concept of a covenant. A covenant is a legal binding agreement. The Living Bible indicates that the new covenant in the bible is placed upon people's hearts, based on a desire to love and serve God, known by all, and is a personal relationship with God. These criteria serve as wonderful models for all relationships. So let it be known:

Whereas we recognize the love, compassion, and care we have for one another. Let it be resolved that a union in this nation is not always recognized legally or practically. Therefore, a covenant made this ____ day of _____, year indicates that the Lord, who is my Savior, has provided a soulmate, a friend, a helper, a confidant.

And this soulmate is my love. S/he is my lifeline in the midst of worry. S/he is my life raft in a sea of turmoil. S/he is my life in the middle of this universe. _____ has a special place in my heart deeper than friends or family, attached along a vessel of joy, an artery of singing, and an aorta of praise.

Know that each of us love the Lord with all our hearts, souls, and minds and shall not let our love strangle the love we have for the Lord. We will serve the Lord, our God, with the beautiful, unique gifts he has upon us bestowed. We will serve him with gladness, hoping that others will recognize our work, but ultimately resting in the assurance that the Master will one day say, "Well done, my good and faithful servants"

Today, in front of each of you, let our love for one another be proclaimed, not searching or needing your approval or permission. For love does not look for external acceptance. It goes forth boldly and rightly.

For, I, _____, love _____. And I, _____, love _____.

Finally, based on our soul salvation, we will build this relationship based on the same principles by which the relationship with our Lord grows: through prayer, praise, study, communion, care, communication, and unconditional agape love.

So today, we make a covenant with the Lord and swear to it that we shall not be unfaithful to this promise. And we swear again, this time by the love for each other, for this love is as much as we have for all.

1 Sam. 20:16-17

(also read Faith)

CHANGE

The only thing that remains the same is change.

We live in a world where we can communicate with someone on the other side of the world within seconds via e-mail, text or video mail. The stock market can rise or fall 200 points or more in any given day. Companies downsize, right size, restructure, reengineer, and even close. The pace in America continues to get faster. Movies can now be streamed, televisions hang flat against the wall, pets are no longer furry, but electronic, cyber dating is the quickest way to meet your next mate, the best brand name computer you buy today is outdated within 3 months, and grocery shopping, dining out, and pharmacy meds are completed online and delivered to your house within an hour. The world is changing and has changed.

Recently after filling up at my local gas station, I forgot to close my gas tank on my vehicle. I started to drive the usual 2 miles home and two or three cars honked their horns at me to indicate that the gas tank door was ajar. I thanked them by waving but kept driving. It was raining heavily outside and I didn't feel like pulling over just to secure the gas cap and close the tank door. Yet, drivers began to drive dangerously just to tell me that the gas door was open. Eventually, I had to pull over and close it because people were crossing into traffic to inform me of this. Yes, I know. I should have been impressed at the good heartedness of these people, but what I realized is that we hate to see anything out of the ordinary.

Change bothers us. It assaults our egos, our comfort zone, and our sanity. These people would have rather put themselves and others in danger to fix something that was not an immediate hindrance, then to let me get home and find it for myself. The gas wasn't going to fall out of the car and the car certainly was running fine. We have this belief that change is dreadful.

Change can be as simple as changing your cologne/perfume. We change our clothes for health reasons and to add variety to our appearance and personality. We change our diets to give our taste buds some variety and diversity. We change our hairstyles to stay updated and current. We download or stream hundreds of songs because we hate to hear the same music over and over again.

Change impacts us on a daily basis. Change is the spice of life. It keeps you vibrant, alive, quick, and alert. Although it may require a lot from us, it can never be said that change is boring.

In fact, I encourage change. Here are some change challenges for you to try:
- Sleep on the opposite side of the bed.
- Listen to a random station on the radio for 2 hours.
- Take another route to work and home.
- Introduce yourself to someone in the supermarket.
- Write with your opposite writing hand for 15 minutes.
- Don't answer the phone for 3 days...let the voicemail get it.
- Walk up the stairs backwards (Please hold on to the rail.)
- Go to the mall with tons of shopping bags in your hand and visit each store. (Watch how much attention you get.)
- Send e-mails to all of your e-mail buddies with just the word *Change* in it.

(also read Choices)

END

All good things must come to an end.

On your mark, get set, GO! These famous words are echoed by children across thousands of playgrounds. More importantly, these are the words you should whisper to yourself when you wake up every morning! Yet, there are times when we must also go to the other end of the spectrum and realize things need to end.

We are a society that overeats, overindulges, overspends, watches a tv with over 1000 stations, works two and three jobs, spends little time with our children, and works at jobs that are too stressful and pay too little… this must end. We need to find a standard of living that is acceptable. And if it is not possible in today's market, we must exercise our voting power and put politicians in office who will secure this status for us.

Take up courage and end abusive, non-supportive, emotionally hurtful relationships.

Find the chutzpah and end lopsided, unfulfilling friendships.

Search for employment that is life-sustaining and purpose-centered.

End years at your dead-end job!

Each of us must embrace the *end or mend* philosophy. If you can't end it, you must mend it! You must fix what is broken. If you have been in dysfunctional relationships for too long, mend or end. If you hate your job, mend or end. If your siblings don't do their part in family gatherings, outings, and decisions, mend or end.

Now is the time. Today is all you have! You have the power to mend or end. If you must bring something to an end, make peace with your decision and go forward with grace, courage and finality.

The universe will always support what is healthiest, life giving, and true for you!

(also read Joy)

LIFE

The meaning of life is to give life meaning.

OFFICE OF HUMAN RESOURCES

Job Title: Human Being

Department: Your Community, City, State, Nation, or World

Job Duties: The human being will live up to their ultimate potential, help others along the way and do some, if not all of the following: Enjoy a sunset. Smell the roses. Fly a kite. Build a miniature plane. Learn another language. Travel abroad. Appreciate a bubble bath. Be debt free. Love someone. Let someone love you. Don't rake the leaves. Listen to your children. Listen to your parents. Listen to your grandparents. Listen to your friends. Listen to your pastor. Listen to life. Examine a grain of sand. Make a snowman. Visit a forest. Call out sick. Give a wrapped gift for no reason. Believe in the possibilities. Play in the rain. Ask for forgiveness. Fly. Remember good times. Drink lemonade. Go to a community theater production. Play hide and seek with your partner. Read a Pulitzer Prize winning novel even if you don't understand it. Write a poem. Pray. Breath. Laugh. Go to the arcade and give a child four quarters. Be powerless for a day. Change your attitude. Say thank you. Say please. Play checkers. Sing in the shower. Dance naked. Raise children who care. Listen for the harmony. Make a melody. Skip rocks on a lake. Believe in Santa Claus again. Go ice skating in July. Give love on the holidays. Throw a friendship party. Don't postpone joy!

Minimum Qualifications: A heart, soul, and mind that is determined to do more and be more.

Salary Range: Joy to Sorrow commensurate on experience.

Immediate Supervisor: The Almighty

Closing Date: Death

Probationary Period: A lifetime

To Apply: Complete and submit a childhood, an education, a purpose, a plan, some goals, some friends, some enemies, some successes, some failures, some good times, some bad times, some lost loves, some pain, some pleasure, and some hopes.

Life is an Equal Opportunity Employer.
Life does not discriminate.
Life employs you to take
the blessings with the burdens,
the anguish with the happiness,
the rich with the poor,
the friends with the foes,
and the chaos with the peace.

(also read Fly)

(YOUR WORD GOES HERE)
Quote here...

Explain why this word is so powerful. How has it changed your life?

How can it improve someone's life?

Email me at 30mostpowerfulwords@gmail.com

I await your words.

Godspeed to you.

Made in the USA
Coppell, TX
12 February 2021